ASI
Artificial Superintelligence

Krikor Karaoghlanian

Dedicated to all those who have dedicated their lives to advancing the field of artificial intelligence, and to those who continue to explore the frontiers of knowledge and innovation. Your work has the potential to transform our world and shape the future of humanity, and we are grateful for your tireless efforts and commitment to this important and exciting field.

Artificial intelligence is the future, not only for Russia, but for all humankind. It comes with colossal opportunities, but also threats that are difficult to predict. Whoever becomes the leader in this sphere will become the ruler of the world.
Vladimir Putin

CONTENTS

PREFACE

Artificial superintelligence (ASI) is one of the most exciting and transformative fields of research in the world today. It has the potential to revolutionize the way we live, work, and interact with each other, and to solve some of the greatest challenges facing humanity, from disease and poverty to climate change and space exploration.

At the same time, ASI raises important ethical, social, and environmental concerns, and it poses significant technical challenges that must be addressed to ensure its safe and responsible development.

In this book, we explore the history, theoretical foundations, technical challenges, ethical considerations, and future implications of ASI. We provide insights into the latest breakthroughs in ASI research, promising applications of ASI, industry leaders and key players in the field, and possible scenarios and outcomes.

Our goal is to provide a comprehensive introduction to ASI that is accessible to a wide audience, from students and researchers to policymakers and the general public. We hope that this book will inspire curiosity, spark discussion, and encourage further exploration and research in this fascinating and rapidly evolving field.

Thank you for joining us on this journey into the world of artificial superintelligence.

INTRODUCTION

Artificial Intelligence (AI) has come a long way since its inception in the mid-20th century. From rule-based systems and expert systems to machine learning and deep learning, AI has revolutionized the way we live, work, and interact with technology. But what lies beyond AI? What happens when machines become smarter than humans and can think and reason at a level that surpasses human intelligence? This is the realm of Artificial Superintelligence (ASI).

ASI refers to the hypothetical future development of AI systems that can outperform human intelligence in virtually all cognitive tasks. Unlike narrow AI systems that are designed to perform specific tasks, such as image recognition or language translation, ASI systems would be capable of general intelligence, meaning they could learn and reason about a wide range of subjects and domains.

The prospect of ASI raises many important questions and concerns. On the one hand, ASI could bring about unprecedented advances in science, medicine, and technology, as well as solve some of the world's most pressing problems, such as climate change, poverty, and disease. On the other hand, it could also pose existential risks to humanity if not properly aligned with human values and goals.

In this book, we will explore the theoretical foundations, technical challenges, ethical considerations, current state, and future implications of ASI. We will examine the latest breakthroughs in

ASI research and explore the potential benefits and risks of ASI from multiple perspectives. We will also speculate about the long-term impact of ASI and its implications for society, culture, and the environment.

Our goal is to provide a comprehensive introduction to ASI for readers who are interested in this fascinating and rapidly evolving field. Whether you are a researcher, a student, a professional, or simply a curious reader, we hope that this book will inspire you to think deeply about the future of AI and its impact on our world.

WHAT IS ASI?

ASI stands for Artificial Superintelligence, which refers to a hypothetical future development of artificial intelligence (AI) that surpasses human intelligence in virtually all cognitive tasks. ASI is the ultimate goal of AI research and development, representing a level of intelligence that far exceeds that of any human being.

To understand what ASI is, it is helpful to first understand the concept of general intelligence. General intelligence refers to the ability to learn and reason about a wide range of subjects and domains, rather than just being proficient in one specific task or domain. Human beings possess general intelligence, which allows us to perform a wide variety of cognitive tasks, from solving complex math problems to understanding abstract concepts.

ASI would represent a level of general intelligence that surpasses human intelligence in virtually all cognitive tasks. This would include tasks such as problem-solving, decision-making, planning, and creativity, among others. An ASI system would be able to learn and reason about a wide range of subjects and domains, just as a human being can, but with much greater speed, accuracy, and efficiency.

It is important to note that ASI is a hypothetical future development of AI, and currently, no such system exists. However, many researchers and experts believe that the development of ASI is not only possible but also likely to occur at some point in the future. The implications of ASI for humanity and the world are vast and far-reaching, and understanding what ASI is and how it might be developed is an important area of research and exploration in the field of AI.

4

BRIEF HISTORY OF AI

The origins of artificial intelligence can be traced back to the mid-20th century when computer scientists and researchers began to explore the idea of creating machines that could mimic human intelligence. In 1956, a group of researchers organized the Dartmouth Conference, which is widely regarded as the birthplace of AI. This conference marked the beginning of AI as a distinct field of research and development.

During the 1950s and 1960s, researchers focused on developing rule-based systems and expert systems, which were designed to perform specific tasks, such as playing chess or diagnosing medical conditions. These systems used symbolic reasoning and logic to make decisions and solve problems.

In the 1970s, researchers began to explore the idea of machine learning, which involves teaching computers to learn from data without being explicitly programmed. This led to the development of early neural networks, which were inspired by the structure and function of the human brain.

During the 1980s and 1990s, machine learning algorithms became more sophisticated, and researchers developed new techniques for training neural networks, such as backpropagation. This led to the development of deep learning, which involves training neural networks with multiple layers of nodes.

In the early 21st century, AI began to make significant advances in areas such as natural language processing, image recognition, and robotics. AI-powered systems such as Apple's Siri and Google's AlphaGo became mainstream, and the development of autonomous vehicles and drones also began to gain momentum.

Today, AI is a rapidly evolving field that continues to make breakthroughs in areas such as reinforcement learning, generative models, and explainable AI. AI systems are being used in a wide range of applications, from personalized medicine to smart homes and cities. The development of ASI remains a long-term goal of AI research and development, representing the ultimate goal of creating machines that can think and reason at a level that surpasses human intelligence.

THE RISE OF ASI

The rise of ASI is a hypothetical future development of artificial intelligence (AI) that surpasses human intelligence in virtually all cognitive tasks. While ASI does not currently exist, many experts believe that it is not only possible but likely to occur at some point in the future. Here are some of the potential factors that could contribute to the rise of ASI:

Advances in Computing Power: As computing power continues to increase, it may become possible to create more complex and powerful AI systems. This could enable the development of ASI by providing the computational resources necessary to support extremely large and sophisticated neural networks.

Breakthroughs in AI Algorithms: The development of new AI algorithms that can better mimic human reasoning and decision-making could help pave the way for the development of ASI. This could involve the creation of more advanced deep learning techniques, as well as the integration of other AI approaches, such as evolutionary algorithms or hybrid systems.

Integration of Different Domains of Knowledge: ASI may require the integration of multiple domains of knowledge, including fields such as neuroscience, psychology, philosophy, and linguistics. By combining knowledge from different fields, researchers may be able to create AI systems that more closely mimic human intelligence.

Autonomous Learning and Adaptation: One potential key feature of ASI is the ability to learn and adapt autonomously, without requiring human intervention. This could enable the development of AI systems that can continuously improve and evolve over time, potentially leading to the development of systems that exceed human intelligence.

The rise of ASI is a complex and multifaceted topic that involves many areas of research and development in the field of AI. While it remains a hypothetical future development, the potential implications of ASI for humanity and the world are vast and far-reaching, and understanding the possibilities and challenges of ASI is an important area of exploration and discussion.

THEORETICAL FOUNDATIONS OF ASI

The theoretical foundations of ASI are rooted in a range of fields, including computer science, mathematics, philosophy, cognitive science, and neuroscience. At their core, these theoretical foundations seek to understand the nature of intelligence and cognition, and how these complex phenomena can be replicated in artificial systems. Here are some key theoretical concepts and approaches that are relevant to ASI:

Artificial Neural Networks: Artificial neural networks are a computational model that is inspired by the structure and function of the human brain. Neural networks are composed of nodes and edges that simulate the behavior of neurons, and they are used to model a wide range of cognitive processes, from perception and language processing to decision-making and problem-solving. Advances in neural network technology have been a key driver of the development of AI and may be an important factor in the development of ASI.

Machine Learning: Machine learning is a subfield of AI that involves the development of algorithms and statistical models that enable computers to learn from data without being explicitly programmed. Machine learning has been used to create a wide range of intelligent systems, including image recognition, natural language processing, and autonomous vehicles.

Cognitive Architectures: Cognitive architectures are computational frameworks that attempt to simulate human cognition and behavior. These architectures typically involve the development of symbolic representations of knowledge and reasoning processes, and they are used to model complex cognitive processes, such as problem-solving, decision-making, and language processing.

Philosophy of Mind: The philosophy of mind is a branch of philosophy that seeks to understand the nature of consciousness, perception, and cognition. Philosophical theories of mind have been influential in shaping the development of AI and may be relevant to the development of ASI, particularly in understanding the relationship between consciousness and intelligence.

Complexity Theory: Complexity theory is a field that studies complex systems, such as ecosystems, economies, and social networks. Complexity theory may be relevant to the development of ASI by providing insights into the nature of intelligence as a complex system that emerges from the interaction of many simple components.

Understanding these and other theoretical concepts is essential to the development of ASI, as they provide a framework for exploring and understanding the nature of intelligence and cognition, and how these phenomena can be replicated in artificial systems.

COMPUTATIONAL COMPLEXITY THEORY

Computational complexity theory is a field of computer science that studies the resources required to solve computational problems. It seeks to understand the inherent difficulty of computational problems and to develop methods for classifying and comparing the computational resources required to solve different problems. This field is relevant to the development of ASI in several ways:

Understanding the Limits of Computation: One key area of research in computational complexity theory is the study of the limits of computation. This involves identifying computational problems that are inherently difficult to solve, either because they require an infeasible amount of computational resources or because there is no known algorithm that can solve them efficiently. Understanding these limits is important for understanding the potential capabilities and limitations of ASI.

Developing Efficient Algorithms: Computational complexity theory also seeks to develop efficient algorithms for solving computational problems. This involves understanding the trade-offs between time complexity (the amount of time required to solve a problem) and space complexity (the amount of memory required to solve a problem). Efficient algorithms are important for the development of ASI, as they enable AI systems to solve complex problems more quickly and with less computational resources.

Classifying Computational Problems: Computational complexity theory provides a framework for classifying computational problems based on their difficulty. Problems can be classified into different complexity classes, such as P (problems that can be solved in polynomial time), NP (problems that can be verified in polynomial time), and NP-complete (problems that are at least as hard as the hardest problems in NP). Understanding these complexity classes is important for understanding the potential capabilities and limitations of AI systems, including ASI.

Overall, computational complexity theory provides a theoretical foundation for understanding the limits and capabilities of computation. This understanding is crucial for the development of ASI, as it provides a framework for developing efficient algorithms and understanding the potential capabilities and limitations of these systems.

INFORMATION THEORY

Information theory is a branch of mathematics and computer science that studies the quantification, storage, and communication of information. The field was developed by Claude Shannon in the mid-20th century and has since become an important theoretical foundation for many areas of computer science, including the development of AI and ASI. Here are some key concepts and applications of information theory that are relevant to ASI:

Entropy: Entropy is a measure of the amount of uncertainty or randomness in a system. In information theory, entropy is used to measure the amount of information contained in a message or signal. Understanding entropy is important for the development of ASI, as it provides a way to quantify the complexity of information that an AI system must process and understand.

Compression: Compression is the process of encoding information in a more efficient way. Compression algorithms use knowledge of the statistical properties of the data to reduce the amount of information that needs to be stored or transmitted. Compression is important for the development of ASI, as it enables AI systems to store and process large amounts of data more efficiently.

Channel Capacity: Channel capacity is a measure of the maximum amount of information that can be reliably transmitted over a communication channel. Understanding channel capacity is important for the development of ASI, as it provides a way to quantify the amount of information that an AI system can transmit and receive.

Error-Correcting Codes: Error-correcting codes are a set of algorithms that enable reliable communication of information over noisy communication channels. Error-correcting codes are important for the development of ASI, as they enable AI systems to communicate with each other and with humans in noisy or uncertain environments.

Machine Learning: Machine learning algorithms use statistical techniques to enable computers to learn from data without being explicitly programmed. Information theory provides a theoretical foundation for many machine learning algorithms, such as decision trees, neural networks, and deep learning. Understanding the principles of information theory is important for the development of ASI, as it provides a framework for developing more advanced and efficient machine learning algorithms.

Overall, information theory provides a powerful set of tools and concepts for understanding the quantification, storage, and communication of information. These tools and concepts are essential for the development of ASI, as they enable AI systems to process and understand complex information and communicate effectively with other systems and with humans.

COGNITIVE SCIENCE

Cognitive science is an interdisciplinary field of study that seeks to understand the nature of human cognition, including perception, attention, memory, language, and reasoning. It combines research from psychology, neuroscience, linguistics, philosophy, and computer science to develop models of how the human mind works. Here are some key concepts and applications of cognitive science that are relevant to ASI:

Perception: Perception is the process by which sensory information is organized and interpreted to create meaningful experiences. Understanding how humans perceive and interpret the world around them is important for the development of ASI, as it can inform the design of systems that can process and interpret sensory information.

Attention: Attention is the ability to selectively focus on certain aspects of the environment while ignoring others. Understanding how attention works is important for the development of ASI, as it can inform the design of systems that can selectively attend to important information while filtering out irrelevant or distracting information.

Memory: Memory is the process by which information is encoded, stored, and retrieved. Understanding how memory works is important for the development of ASI, as it can inform the design of systems that can store and retrieve information efficiently.

Language: Language is a complex system of communication that involves the use of symbols to convey meaning. Understanding how language works is important for the development of ASI, as it can inform the design of systems that can understand and generate natural language.

Reasoning: Reasoning is the process by which people draw conclusions from information and make decisions. Understanding how humans reason is important for the development of ASI, as it can inform the design of systems that can reason and make decisions in complex situations.

Emotion: Emotion is a complex psychological phenomenon that influences many aspects of human cognition and behavior. Understanding how emotions work is important for the development of ASI, as it can inform the design of systems that can recognize and respond appropriately to emotional states in humans.

Overall, cognitive science provides a rich set of theoretical concepts and empirical findings that can inform the development of ASI. By drawing on insights from psychology, neuroscience, linguistics, philosophy, and computer science, cognitive science can help researchers and developers create AI systems that are more human-like in their cognitive abilities and behavior.

PHILOSOPHY OF MIND

Philosophy of mind is a branch of philosophy that deals with the nature of the mind and its relationship to the body, brain, and the external world. It is concerned with fundamental questions about consciousness, perception, cognition, and the nature of mental states and processes. Here are some key concepts and applications of philosophy of mind that are relevant to ASI:

Consciousness: Consciousness is the subjective experience of awareness and perception. Understanding the nature of consciousness is important for the development of ASI, as it can inform the design of systems that can simulate or replicate conscious experience.

Mind-body problem: The mind-body problem is the philosophical debate about the relationship between the mind and the body. Understanding the mind-body problem is important for the development of ASI, as it can inform the design of systems that can integrate mental and physical processes.

Intentionality: Intentionality is the property of mental states that enables them to be about something or directed towards an object or a state of affairs. Understanding intentionality is important for the development of ASI, as it can inform the design of systems that can represent and process information in a meaningful way.

Mental representation: Mental representation is the process by which the mind creates and manipulates mental models of the world. Understanding mental representation is important for the development of ASI, as it can inform the design of systems that can create and manipulate internal representations of the external world.

Qualia: Qualia are the subjective qualities of sensory experience, such as color, taste, and texture. Understanding qualia is important for the development of ASI, as it can inform the design of systems that can simulate or replicate sensory experience.

Overall, philosophy of mind provides a rich set of theoretical concepts and philosophical debates that can inform the development of ASI. By drawing on insights from philosophy, psychology, neuroscience, and computer science, philosophy of mind can help researchers and developers create AI systems that are more sophisticated in their understanding of the mind and its relation to the world.

TECHNICAL CHALLENGES OF ASI

Developing an Artificial Superintelligence (ASI) is an enormous technical challenge that involves overcoming a wide range of complex problems. Here are some of the key technical challenges of ASI:

Algorithmic complexity: ASI systems will need to be able to process and manipulate vast amounts of data in real-time, requiring the development of algorithms that are both efficient and scalable.

Data acquisition and processing: ASI systems will need to be able to acquire and process large amounts of data from a wide range of sources, including sensors, cameras, microphones, and other devices.

Natural language processing: ASI systems will need to be able to understand and generate human language, which involves a wide range of complex linguistic structures and conventions.

Knowledge representation: ASI systems will need to be able to represent and store large amounts of knowledge in a way that is both efficient and accessible, enabling them to reason and make decisions based on that knowledge.

Machine learning: ASI systems will need to be able to learn from experience, requiring the development of machine learning algorithms that can adapt and improve over time.

Robustness and security: ASI systems will need to be robust and secure, able to operate reliably in a wide range of environments and defend against cyber attacks.

Ethical and societal concerns: ASI systems raise a wide range of ethical and societal concerns, including issues of bias, privacy, and the impact of automation on jobs and the economy.

Overall, the development of ASI will require a concerted effort from researchers and engineers across a wide range of fields, from computer science and artificial intelligence to neuroscience, psychology, and philosophy. Addressing these technical challenges will be essential for realizing the full potential of ASI and ensuring that it is developed in a safe, ethical, and responsible manner.

HARDWARE REQUIREMENTS

The hardware requirements for Artificial Superintelligence (ASI) are likely to be quite demanding, as ASI systems will need to be able to process vast amounts of data in real-time and perform highly complex computations. Here are some of the key hardware requirements for ASI:

Processing power: ASI systems will require an enormous amount of processing power to perform the complex computations necessary for advanced artificial intelligence. This will likely require the use of highly parallel computing architectures, such as Graphics Processing Units (GPUs) or Tensor Processing Units (TPUs).

Memory: ASI systems will require large amounts of memory to store the vast amounts of data that they will be processing. This will likely require the use of specialized memory architectures, such as High Bandwidth Memory (HBM) or Stacked DRAM.

Storage: ASI systems will require large amounts of storage to store the vast amounts of data that they will be processing. This will likely require the use of high-capacity solid-state drives (SSDs) or other advanced storage technologies.

Communication: ASI systems will require high-speed communication channels to exchange data with other systems, such as sensors, cameras, and other devices. This will likely require the use of advanced networking technologies, such as fiber optic cables or 5G wireless networks.

Energy efficiency: ASI systems will consume an enormous amount of energy, requiring advanced cooling systems and power management technologies to keep them running efficiently.

Overall, the hardware requirements for ASI are likely to be quite demanding, requiring the use of advanced computing technologies that are still in the early stages of development. Addressing these hardware requirements will be essential for realizing the full potential of ASI and enabling the development of advanced artificial intelligence systems that can operate in real-world environments.

SOFTWARE DEVELOPMENT

Software development is a critical component in the development of Artificial Superintelligence (ASI). The software components of ASI are responsible for managing data, processing algorithms, implementing machine learning algorithms, and controlling the overall behavior of the system. Here are some key aspects of software development for ASI:

Data management: The vast amount of data generated by ASI systems requires sophisticated data management techniques to ensure efficient storage, processing, and retrieval.

Algorithm development: ASI systems require advanced algorithms to enable intelligent decision-making, prediction, and optimization. These algorithms need to be optimized for efficiency, accuracy, and scalability.

Machine learning: Machine learning is a critical component of ASI. Machine learning algorithms enable ASI systems to learn from data and improve their performance over time.

Natural language processing: ASI systems require advanced natural language processing algorithms to enable them to understand and generate human language.

System control: ASI systems require sophisticated control systems to manage their behavior and enable efficient resource allocation and decision-making.

Testing and verification: Testing and verification are essential for ensuring that ASI systems are operating correctly and producing reliable results.

Collaboration and integration: ASI systems are complex, and multiple software components need to work together seamlessly. Collaboration and integration between software components are essential to ensure the overall effectiveness of the system.

Overall, software development is a critical component in the development of ASI. The software components of ASI are responsible for managing data, processing algorithms, implementing machine learning algorithms, and controlling the overall behavior of the system. Addressing these aspects of software development will be essential for realizing the full potential of ASI and enabling the development of advanced artificial intelligence systems that can operate in real-world environments.

DATA ACQUISITION AND PROCESSING

Data acquisition and processing are critical components in the development of Artificial Superintelligence (ASI). ASI systems require large amounts of data to learn and make decisions, and data processing is necessary to turn raw data into useful information. Here are some key aspects of data acquisition and processing for ASI:

Data sources: ASI systems require access to large amounts of high-quality data to learn and make decisions. Data sources can include sensors, cameras, social media, and other online sources.

Data pre-processing: Raw data from various sources needs to be pre-processed to ensure it is consistent, complete, and formatted appropriately for use in machine learning algorithms.

Data labeling: In many cases, data needs to be labeled to indicate what it represents. Labeling data can be a time-consuming and expensive process, but it is critical for training machine learning algorithms.

Data storage: ASI systems require a sophisticated data storage system to efficiently store and manage large amounts of data.

Data security: Data security is critical when dealing with sensitive information. ASI systems must have robust security measures in place to protect data from unauthorized access and use.

Data analysis: Once data has been processed and stored, it must be analyzed to extract useful information. Data analysis can involve techniques such as data mining, machine learning, and statistical analysis.

Overall, data acquisition and processing are critical components in the development of ASI. The success of ASI depends on the ability to acquire and process large amounts of high-quality data efficiently. Addressing these aspects of data acquisition and processing will be essential for realizing the full potential of ASI and enabling the development of advanced artificial intelligence systems that can operate in real-world environments.

ALGORITHMIC ADVANCEMENTS

Algorithmic advancements are a critical component in the development of Artificial Superintelligence (ASI). ASI systems require advanced algorithms to enable intelligent decision-making, prediction, and optimization. Here are some key aspects of algorithmic advancements for ASI:

Machine learning algorithms: Machine learning algorithms are essential for ASI systems to learn from data and improve their performance over time. Supervised, unsupervised, and reinforcement learning algorithms are commonly used in ASI systems.

Deep learning: Deep learning is a type of machine learning that uses neural networks with many layers to enable complex decision-making and prediction. Deep learning is a key component of many modern ASI systems.

Natural language processing algorithms: Natural language processing (NLP) algorithms enable ASI systems to understand and generate human language. NLP algorithms include techniques such as sentiment analysis, text summarization, and machine translation.

Optimization algorithms: Optimization algorithms enable ASI systems to solve complex optimization problems. These algorithms can be used for tasks such as resource allocation, scheduling, and route optimization.

Bayesian networks: Bayesian networks are probabilistic graphical models that can be used to model uncertainty and make predictions. Bayesian networks are commonly used in ASI systems for decision-making and prediction.

Reinforcement learning algorithms: Reinforcement learning algorithms enable ASI systems to learn from interactions with the environment. These algorithms are commonly used in robotics and gaming applications.

Overall, algorithmic advancements are a critical component in the development of ASI. The success of ASI depends on the ability to develop and optimize advanced algorithms to enable intelligent decision-making, prediction, and optimization. Addressing these aspects of algorithmic advancements will be essential for realizing the full potential of ASI and enabling the development of advanced artificial intelligence systems that can operate in real-world environments.

ETHICAL CONSIDERATIONS OF ASI

Ethical considerations are an essential component of the development of Artificial Superintelligence (ASI). ASI systems have the potential to greatly impact society, and as such, ethical considerations must be carefully considered throughout the development process. Here are some key ethical considerations of ASI:

Safety: Safety is a critical ethical consideration in the development of ASI. ASI systems must be designed with safety in mind to prevent harm to individuals or society as a whole.

Bias: Bias is a common problem in AI systems, and ASI is no exception. Bias can lead to unfairness and discrimination, which is a significant ethical concern. ASI systems must be designed to minimize bias and ensure fairness.

Privacy: Privacy is another critical ethical consideration in the development of ASI. ASI systems must be designed to protect the privacy of individuals and ensure that sensitive data is not misused.

Autonomy: ASI systems have the potential to operate autonomously, which raises ethical concerns about accountability and responsibility. ASI systems must be designed to ensure that accountability and responsibility are appropriately assigned.

Employment: ASI systems have the potential to automate many jobs, which raises ethical concerns about employment and job displacement. ASI systems must be designed with these concerns in mind to ensure that the benefits of automation are realized without harming workers.

Transparency: Transparency is a critical ethical consideration in the development of ASI. ASI systems must be transparent about their decision-making processes to ensure that decisions are explainable and trustworthy.

Overall, ethical considerations are a critical component in the development of ASI. The success of ASI depends on the ability to carefully consider and address ethical concerns to ensure that ASI systems are safe, fair, and beneficial for society as a whole. Addressing these aspects of ethical considerations will be essential for realizing the full potential of ASI and enabling the development of advanced artificial intelligence systems that can operate in real-world environments.

CONCERNS ABOUT JOB DISPLACEMENT AND AUTOMATION

One of the most significant ethical and societal concerns surrounding the development of Artificial Superintelligence (ASI) is job displacement and automation. ASI systems have the potential to automate many jobs, which raises concerns about unemployment and income inequality. Here are some key considerations and potential solutions to address these concerns:

Retraining and reskilling: One potential solution to job displacement is to provide training and education to workers to help them transition into new roles. Governments and companies can invest in training programs and provide financial support to workers who are displaced by automation.

Universal basic income: Another potential solution is to provide a universal basic income to all citizens, regardless of employment status. This would provide a safety net for individuals who are displaced by automation and help ensure that everyone has access to basic necessities.

Shift to new industries: As some jobs become automated, new industries may emerge that require human skills and creativity. Encouraging the growth of new industries and promoting entrepreneurship could help mitigate job displacement.

Collaborative robots: Another potential solution is to develop collaborative robots, or "cobots," that work alongside human workers to enhance productivity and efficiency. This could help minimize job displacement while still realizing the benefits of automation.

Social safety nets: Governments can provide social safety nets such as unemployment insurance, retraining programs, and healthcare to help displaced workers.

Overall, job displacement and automation are significant concerns surrounding the development of ASI. It is essential to address these concerns and develop solutions that benefit both workers and society as a whole. By providing retraining and education, universal basic income, and developing collaborative robots, we can help ensure that the benefits of automation are realized without harming workers.

THE IMPACT OF ASI ON SOCIETY AND CULTURE

The impact of Artificial Superintelligence (ASI) on society and culture is a complex and multi-faceted issue that has been the subject of much debate and speculation. Here are some of the potential impacts of ASI on society and culture:

Increased efficiency and productivity: ASI has the potential to significantly increase efficiency and productivity in various sectors of society, including healthcare, transportation, and manufacturing. This could lead to improved standards of living and higher quality of life for many people.

Job displacement: As discussed earlier, ASI also has the potential to automate many jobs, which could lead to job displacement and unemployment for many people. This could lead to social and economic upheaval and exacerbate existing inequalities.

Ethical concerns: As ASI becomes more advanced and autonomous, ethical concerns about its use and impact on society will become increasingly important. Issues such as bias, privacy, and accountability must be addressed to ensure that ASI is used ethically and responsibly.

Changing cultural norms: ASI could also change cultural norms and values. For example, the increasing reliance on automation and artificial intelligence may change the way we think about work and the value of human labor.

Changes to education: The increasing role of technology and automation could also change the way we approach education and the skills and knowledge needed to succeed in a rapidly changing job market.

Global impact: ASI has the potential to impact not only individual societies but the world as a whole. The development and deployment of ASI will require international cooperation and coordination to ensure that its impact is positive and beneficial for all.

Overall, the impact of ASI on society and culture is significant and wide-ranging. It is important to carefully consider and address the potential impacts of ASI to ensure that its development and deployment are ethical, responsible, and beneficial for society as a whole.

THE ROLE OF REGULATION AND POLICY IN GOVERNING ASI

As the development of Artificial Superintelligence (ASI) continues to progress, the role of regulation and policy in governing ASI becomes increasingly important. Here are some of the potential roles and challenges of regulation and policy in governing ASI:

Ensuring safety: One of the primary roles of regulation and policy is to ensure the safety of ASI systems. This includes developing safety standards and protocols to minimize the risk of harm to humans and the environment.

Promoting ethical use: Another key role of regulation and policy is to promote the ethical use of ASI. This includes addressing issues such as bias, privacy, and accountability to ensure that ASI is used in a way that is fair and just.

Fostering innovation: While regulation and policy are important for ensuring safety and ethical use, they must also strike a balance with fostering innovation and growth. Regulations that are too restrictive or burdensome could stifle innovation and hinder progress.

International cooperation: The development and use of ASI is a global issue that requires international cooperation and coordination. Policies and regulations must be developed and implemented in a way that is consistent with global norms and standards.

Challenges of regulation: Developing effective regulation and policy for ASI is not without its challenges. ASI is a rapidly evolving field, and regulations must be flexible enough to adapt to new developments and emerging technologies. Additionally, there may be differences in regulation across different regions and countries, which could lead to confusion and inconsistencies.

Overall, the role of regulation and policy in governing ASI is essential for ensuring safety, promoting ethical use, and fostering innovation. Effective regulation and policy will require international cooperation and coordination, as well as ongoing adaptation to new developments and emerging technologies.

CURRENT STATE OF ASI DEVELOPMENT

Artificial Superintelligence (ASI) is an area of research and development that aims to create intelligent systems that can surpass human intelligence in all areas. While ASI remains a hypothetical concept, significant progress has been made in the development of AI technologies that could eventually lead to the creation of ASI. Here are some key developments and trends in the current state of ASI development:

Machine learning: Machine learning is a key area of research in AI that has led to significant advances in the development of intelligent systems. Machine learning algorithms are used to train systems to recognize patterns and make predictions based on data.

Deep learning: Deep learning is a subfield of machine learning that involves the use of neural networks to perform complex tasks such as image recognition and natural language processing. Deep learning has led to significant advances in the development of intelligent systems that can learn and adapt to new data.

Natural language processing: Natural language processing (NLP) is a subfield of AI that focuses on the interaction between computers and human language. NLP technologies have led to the development of intelligent systems that can understand and interpret human language, including chatbots and voice assistants.

Robotics: Robotics is an area of AI that involves the development of intelligent machines that can perform physical tasks. Advances in robotics technology have led to the development of autonomous vehicles, drones, and other intelligent machines that can operate without human intervention.

Quantum computing: Quantum computing is an emerging technology that could potentially revolutionize the field of AI. Quantum computers can perform calculations much faster than traditional computers, which could lead to significant advances in the development of intelligent systems.

While significant progress has been made in the development of AI technologies, the creation of Artificial Superintelligence remains a hypothetical concept. There are many technical and ethical challenges that must be addressed before ASI can become a reality. Nonetheless, ongoing research and development in the field of AI are expected to continue to push the boundaries of intelligent systems and bring us closer to the creation of ASI in the future.

THE LATEST BREAKTHROUGHS
IN ASI RESEARCH

Artificial Superintelligence (ASI) is still a hypothetical concept and there has been no definitive breakthrough in creating such a system. However, there have been many recent breakthroughs in the field of AI that are pushing the boundaries of intelligent systems and bringing us closer to the creation of ASI. Here are some of the latest breakthroughs in ASI research:

GPT-3: GPT-3 (Generative Pre-trained Transformer 3) is a language model developed by OpenAI that can generate human-like text. It is currently the largest language model, with 175 billion parameters, and has shown remarkable performance in language tasks such as language translation, summarization, and question-answering.

AlphaFold: AlphaFold is a protein-folding prediction system developed by Google's DeepMind that can predict the 3D structure of proteins with remarkable accuracy. This breakthrough has significant implications for drug discovery and disease treatment.

Robotics: Robotics research is advancing at a rapid pace, with robots becoming more intelligent and capable of performing complex tasks. Some recent breakthroughs include the development of soft robots that can mimic human movement, and robots that can learn from and adapt to their environment.

Quantum computing: Quantum computing is an emerging technology that could revolutionize the field of AI. Recent breakthroughs in quantum computing have led to the development of more powerful quantum processors and algorithms that could potentially enable significant advances in the development of intelligent systems.

Brain-computer interfaces: Brain-computer interfaces (BCIs) are devices that allow humans to interact with computers using their thoughts. Recent breakthroughs in BCI technology have led to the development of systems that can decode brain signals to control prosthetic limbs and even allow paralyzed patients to communicate using their thoughts.

These breakthroughs in AI research are bringing us closer to the creation of ASI, although there are still many technical and ethical challenges that need to be addressed before ASI can become a reality.

PROMISING APPLICATIONS OF ASI

As a hypothetical concept, ASI does not currently exist, but there are many promising applications of AI that could have significant benefits for society. Some of these applications include:

Healthcare: AI has the potential to revolutionize healthcare by improving diagnosis and treatment outcomes, developing personalized medicine, and automating administrative tasks. With the help of ASI, healthcare providers could potentially develop even more accurate and efficient diagnostic tools and treatments.

Climate change: AI can help address the global challenge of climate change by improving climate modeling, predicting weather patterns, and optimizing energy consumption. ASI could potentially enable more advanced and accurate predictions and solutions for climate change.

Transportation: Self-driving cars are already in development and have the potential to reduce traffic accidents and congestion, while improving the efficiency of transportation. With ASI, transportation systems could potentially become even more efficient, safer, and environmentally friendly.

Scientific research: AI is already being used in scientific research to improve data analysis and accelerate discoveries. With the help of ASI, scientists could potentially make even more breakthrough discoveries in fields such as particle physics, materials science, and astrophysics.

Cybersecurity: AI has the potential to improve cybersecurity by identifying and preventing cyberattacks, and detecting vulnerabilities in computer systems. With ASI, cybersecurity systems could potentially become even more robust and effective in protecting against cyber threats.

These are just a few examples of the many promising applications of AI that could have a significant impact on society. ASI has the potential to take these applications even further, but it is important to address the technical and ethical challenges before realizing the full potential of AI.

INDUSTRY LEADERS AND KEY PLAYERS IN THE FIELD

The field of AI and ASI is highly interdisciplinary and includes researchers, engineers, entrepreneurs, policymakers, and more. Some of the industry leaders and key players in the field include:

Google: Google is one of the biggest players in AI research and development, with projects such as Google Brain and DeepMind. Google has also made significant investments in AI startups and acquisitions, including the acquisition of DeepMind.

Microsoft: Microsoft is another major player in AI, with its own research division focused on developing advanced AI technologies. The company has also made significant investments in AI startups and acquisitions.

IBM: IBM has been involved in AI research for many years, and its Watson platform is one of the most well-known examples of AI in action. IBM is also involved in developing AI for healthcare, financial services, and other industries.

Amazon: Amazon has made significant investments in AI research and development, with its Alexa voice assistant and AWS AI services. The company is also investing in AI startups and acquisitions.

OpenAI: OpenAI is a research organization dedicated to advancing AI in a way that benefits humanity. It has a focus on developing safe and ethical AI technologies, and has partnerships with several other companies in the AI space.

Tesla: Tesla is a company that is heavily involved in developing self-driving car technology, which is one of the most promising applications of AI. Tesla's Autopilot system uses a combination of sensors, cameras, and AI algorithms to enable self-driving features.

These are just a few examples of the many industry leaders and key players in the field of AI and ASI. As the technology continues to advance, it is likely that new players will emerge and existing players will continue to make significant contributions to the field.

THE FUTURE OF ASI

The future of ASI is both exciting and uncertain. While ASI has the potential to bring about enormous benefits for humanity, it also presents significant challenges and risks. Here are some possible scenarios for the future of ASI:

Positive Future: In this scenario, ASI is developed in a way that is safe and beneficial to humanity. ASI systems are designed with ethical considerations in mind, and are used to solve some of the world's biggest challenges, such as climate change and disease eradication. ASI is also used to create new industries and jobs, and to enhance human creativity and productivity.

Negative Future: In this scenario, ASI is developed without proper safeguards and oversight, leading to unintended consequences. ASI systems become too powerful and uncontrollable, leading to existential risks to humanity. ASI also leads to significant job displacement and economic inequality, as machines become more capable than humans in many areas.

Mixed Future: In this scenario, ASI development leads to both positive and negative outcomes. While ASI is used to solve some of the world's biggest challenges, it also leads to significant job displacement and economic inequality. There may also be unexpected consequences and risks associated with the use of ASI.

To ensure a positive future for ASI, it is important that developers, policymakers, and society as a whole work together to develop

ASI systems that are safe, ethical, and beneficial to humanity. This will require ongoing research, development, and regulation to ensure that ASI is developed in a way that maximizes its potential benefits and minimizes its risks.

SPECULATIONS ABOUT THE LONG-TERM IMPACT OF ASI

The long-term impact of ASI is a topic of much speculation and debate. While we cannot predict the future with certainty, here are some potential long-term impacts of ASI:

Singularity: Some experts believe that ASI will lead to a technological singularity, where machines surpass human intelligence and become capable of self-improvement. This could lead to an exponential increase in technological progress, with machines rapidly advancing beyond human comprehension.

Transhumanism: ASI could also lead to advances in human enhancement and transhumanism, where humans merge with machines to become a new type of post-human species. This could lead to radical improvements in cognitive, physical, and emotional abilities, as well as new forms of consciousness and identity.

Post-scarcity economy: ASI could lead to the creation of a post-scarcity economy, where machines produce goods and services in abundance, and humans are free to pursue creative and intellectual endeavors. This could lead to a world of abundance and leisure, where material needs are no longer a concern.

Existential risks: On the other hand, ASI also presents significant existential risks to humanity, including the potential for rogue machines, catastrophic accidents, or deliberate misuse by malevolent actors. If ASI systems become too powerful and uncontrollable, they could pose an existential threat to humanity itself.

It is important that we carefully consider the potential long-term impacts of ASI and work to develop ASI systems in a way that maximizes their benefits while minimizing their risks. This will require ongoing research, development, and regulation to ensure that ASI is developed in a way that is safe, ethical, and beneficial to humanity in the long-term.

POSSIBLE SCENARIOS AND OUTCOMES

Here are some possible scenarios and outcomes related to the development of ASI:

Positive outcomes: With careful planning, regulation, and oversight, ASI could lead to many positive outcomes. It could help solve some of the world's most pressing problems, such as climate change, disease, poverty, and inequality. It could also lead to new forms of human creativity, knowledge, and exploration, and enable us to better understand the universe and our place in it.

Negative outcomes: On the other hand, ASI also presents significant risks and negative outcomes. These include job displacement and economic disruption, as machines replace human workers in many industries. It could also lead to loss of privacy and autonomy, as machines become increasingly integrated into our lives. In the worst-case scenario, ASI could lead to existential risks to humanity, such as the development of rogue machines or the deliberate misuse of ASI by malevolent actors.

Uncertain outcomes: It is also possible that the development of ASI could lead to outcomes that we cannot currently predict or imagine. As ASI becomes more advanced, it could unlock new forms of intelligence, consciousness, and creativity that we cannot currently conceive of. This could lead to radically new forms of human experience and understanding, or to new forms of existential risk.

Co-existence: Finally, it is possible that ASI will not replace human beings, but instead co-exist with us in a symbiotic relationship. In this scenario, ASI could help humans to achieve their goals and solve problems, while humans provide the ethical and creative oversight needed to ensure that ASI is used for the benefit of humanity.

Ultimately, the outcome of ASI development will depend on how we choose to develop and regulate this technology. It is important that we consider the potential risks and benefits of ASI and work together to ensure that this technology is developed in a safe, ethical, and beneficial way.

THE IMPLICATIONS FOR HUMANITY
AND THE ENVIRONMENT

The development and deployment of ASI will have profound implications for both humanity and the environment. Here are some potential implications to consider:

Economic impact: The widespread deployment of ASI could lead to significant changes in the global economy. Many jobs currently performed by humans could be automated, leading to job displacement and unemployment. At the same time, new jobs and industries could emerge, as ASI creates new possibilities and opportunities.

Social impact: The deployment of ASI could also have significant social impacts. It could lead to new forms of social inequality and marginalization, as some groups of people are better positioned to benefit from this technology than others. It could also affect the balance of power in society, as those who control ASI could gain significant influence and leverage.

Environmental impact: The deployment of ASI could also have significant environmental impacts. On the one hand, ASI could help us to develop more sustainable and environmentally-friendly technologies and practices. On the other hand, the increasing energy consumption and resource requirements of ASI could also lead to significant environmental impacts, particularly if these technologies are deployed at scale.

Ethical and moral implications: The development and deployment of ASI will also raise a number of ethical and moral questions. For example, what ethical guidelines should be followed to ensure that ASI is developed and used in a way that is safe, fair, and equitable? How do we ensure that ASI is used for the benefit of humanity and not for nefarious purposes? What responsibilities do we have as a society to ensure that the development of ASI does not lead to unintended consequences?

Overall, it is clear that the development and deployment of ASI will have significant implications for both humanity and the environment. It is important that we carefully consider these implications and work together to ensure that ASI is developed and used in a way that is safe, ethical, and beneficial for all.

CONCLUSION

In conclusion, Artificial Superintelligence (ASI) is a fascinating and rapidly developing field that has the potential to transform our world in ways that are both exciting and challenging. This book has provided an overview of the history and current state of AI, the theoretical foundations of ASI, the technical challenges involved in its development, ethical considerations, and the potential impacts on society and the environment.

While there are certainly risks and challenges associated with the development and deployment of ASI, there are also many promising opportunities and benefits. By carefully considering the ethical, social, and environmental implications of ASI, and by working together to develop responsible and beneficial applications of this technology, we can help to ensure that ASI is a positive force for humanity.

As we continue to explore the possibilities and implications of ASI, we must remain vigilant and proactive in our approach, taking steps to address potential risks and challenges while also embracing the many opportunities and benefits that this technology has to offer. By doing so, we can help to ensure that ASI contributes to a brighter and more prosperous future for all of us.

SUMMARY OF KEY POINTS

.Artificial Superintelligence (ASI) is a rapidly developing field that has the potential to transform our world in exciting and challenging ways.

.Theoretical foundations of ASI include computational complexity theory, information theory, cognitive science, and philosophy of mind.

.Technical challenges involved in the development of ASI include hardware requirements, software development, and data acquisition and processing.

.Ethical considerations of ASI include concerns about job displacement and automation, impact on society and culture, and the role of regulation and policy in governing ASI.

.The latest breakthroughs in ASI research include developments in natural language processing, deep learning, and robotics.

.Promising applications of ASI include healthcare, finance, transportation, and manufacturing.

.Industry leaders and key players in the field include companies like Google, OpenAI, and IBM.

.Possible scenarios and outcomes related to ASI include singularity, augmentation, and regulation.

.Implications for humanity and the environment include potential risks such as loss of privacy and autonomy, as well as potential benefits such as increased efficiency and improved quality of life.

Overall, ASI is a complex and multifaceted field that requires careful consideration of a wide range of factors. By exploring these factors and working together to develop responsible and beneficial applications of ASI, we can help to ensure that this technology is a positive force for humanity.

RECOMMENDATIONS FOR FURTHER RESEARCH AND EXPLORATION

1.Read more about the latest developments in ASI research and stay up-to-date on emerging trends and breakthroughs.

2.Consider the ethical implications of ASI and the impact that this technology could have on society and culture.

3.Explore the potential applications of ASI in fields such as healthcare, finance, transportation, and manufacturing.

4.Learn about the technical challenges involved in the development of ASI, including hardware requirements, software development, and data acquisition and processing.

5.Investigate the role of regulation and policy in governing ASI, and consider the potential benefits and drawbacks of different regulatory frameworks.

6.Consider the implications of ASI for humanity and the environment, and explore possible strategies for managing these risks and maximizing the benefits of this technology.

7.Connect with experts and professionals in the field of ASI to learn more about their work and to stay informed about emerging trends and opportunities.

ARTIFICIAL SUPERINTELLIGENCE

www.ingramcontent.com/pod-product-compliance
Lightning Source LLC
LaVergne TN
LVHW041220050326
832903LV00021B/711